14X 2/11 √ 3/11

WHY EXTINCTION OCCURS

First published in 2002 by
Grolier Educational
Sherman Turnpike
Danbury, Connecticut 06816
© Quartz Editions 2002

Library of Congress Cataloging-in-Publication Data
Extinct species.
　　　　p. cm.
　 Contents: v. 1. Why extinction occurs - - v. 2. Prehistoric animal life - - v. 3. Fossil
hunting - - v. 4. Extinct mammals - - v. 5. Extinct birds - - v. 6 Extinct underwater life - -
v. 7. Extinct reptiles and amphibians - - v. 8. Extinct invertebrates and plants - - v. 9.
Hominids - - v. 10. Atlas of extinction.
　 Summary: Examines extinct species, including prehistoric man, and discusses why
extinction happens, as well as how information is gathered on species that existed
before humans evolved.
ISBN 0-7172-5564-6 (set) - - ISBN 0-7172-5565-4 (v. 1) - - ISBN 0-7172-5566-2 (v. 2)
- - ISBN 0-7172-5567-0 (v. 3) - - ISBN 0-7172-5568-9 (v. 4) - - ISBN 0-7172-5569-7 (v.
5) - - ISBN 0-7172-5570-0 (v. 6) - - ISBN 0-7172-5571-9 (v. 7) - - ISBN 0-7172-5572-7
(v. 8) - - ISBN 0-7172-5573-5 (v. 9) - - ISBN 0-7172-5574-3 (v. 10)
　 1. Extinction (Biology) - - Juvenile literature. 2. Extinct animals - - Juvenile literature.
[1. Extinction (Biology) 2. Extinct animals.] I. Grolier Educational.

QH78 .E88 2002
578.68 - - dc21　　　　　　　　　　　　　　　　　　　2001055702

Produced by Quartz Editions
Premier House
112 Station Road
Edgware HA8 7BJ
UK

EDITORIAL DIRECTOR: Tamara Green
CREATIVE DIRECTOR: Marilyn Franks
PRINCIPAL ILLUSTRATOR: Neil Lloyd
CONTRIBUTING ILLUSTRATORS: Tony Gibbons, Helen Jones
EDITORIAL CONTRIBUTOR: Graham Coleman

Reprographics by Mullis Morgan, London
Printed in Belgium by Proost

ACKNOWLEDGMENTS

The publishers wish to thank the following for supplying
photographic images for this volume.

Front & back cover t SPL/J.Baum & D.Angus

Page 1t SPL/J.Baum & D.Angus;
p3t SPL/J.Baum & D.Angus;
p9t NHPA/A.N.T.; p10br NHPA/J.Hayward;
p11t NHPA/E.Soder; p11b OSF/K.Wothe;
p13tl NHPA/N.Dennis; p13br NHPA/A.Bannister;
p15tl NHPA/A.Nardi; p15b NHPA/D.Heuclin;
p17tl NHPA/K.Schafer; p17br SPL;
p18b OSF/S.Camazine; p19t NHPA/J.Meech;
p22tr NHPA/D.Heuclin; p22cl NHPA/M.Harvey;
p23tc NHPA/A. & S.Toon; p25bl NHPA/D.Currey;
p25bc NHPA/J.Sauvanet; p25br NHPA/M.Wendler;
p27tl NHPA/M.Harvey; p27bl NHPA/M.Harvey;
p27br NHPA/M.Strange; p28cl NHPA/K.Schafer;
p29tl MEPL/La Samaritaine Catalogue;
p29br NHPA/M.Wendler; p30tr OSF/R.Packwood;
p31br OSF/I.West; p32tr NHPA/M.Walker;
p33tc OSF/I.Cushing; p35t TS/J.Beatty;
p39tl NHPA/Gerard Lacz; p39br OSF/C.Bromhall;
p41t NHPA/M.Bowler; p43tl NHPA/N.Wu;
p43b NHPA/M.Harvey; p44bl OSF/D. & J.Bartlett/Survival
Anglia; p45tc NHPA/A.Rouse.

Abbreviations: Mary Evans Picture Library (MEPL); Natural
History Photographic Agency (NHPA); Oxford Scientific Films
(OSF); Science Photo Library (SPL); Tony Stone (TS); bottom
(b); center (c); left (l); right (r); top (t).

WHY EXTINCTION OCCURS

GROLIER EDUCATIONAL
SHERMAN TURNPIKE, DANBURY, CONNECTICUT 06816

THE COLD TRUTH
How the mammoths managed to thrive during the last Ice Age but then died out is revealed on pages 10-11.

OUT OF FASHION
The rare animal shown here was sometimes taken purely for its pelt. Find out more about this on pages 28-29.

DESERT DOOM
When greater expanses of barren land have formed throughout the world's history, many local species have disappeared, as outlined on pages 34-35.

CONTENTS

WHERE IN THE WORLD?
Turn to pages 20-21 to find out where some exquisite plants and animals have, alas, become extinct and endangered.

BURNED ALIVE
If you turn to pages 22-23, you can find out how the enchanting little creatures *above* were affected by fires.

SUDDEN DISASTERS
Turn to pages 16-17 to discover what may happen to local wildlife when an earthquake occurs. Some animals are actually acute enough to sense such impending disasters before humans.

APPALLING POLLUTION
We now have conclusive proof that smoking chimneys will contaminate the atmosphere for miles around, affecting the health of humans and animals alike, as outlined on pages 32-33.

INTRODUCTION

Sixty-five million years ago, according to widely accepted theory, an asteroid hit the Earth, throwing up the thickest clouds of dust you can imagine from a crater so enormous that it may have covered an area of many thousands of miles. As a result, sunlight was obscured, and a great deal of vegetation died out. There was therefore not enough food for those dinosaurs that were plant-eaters; and once they had declined in number, the meat-eating dinosaurs went hungry. Dinosaurs thus became extinct, along with many other life forms that existed at the end of Cretaceous times.

Scientists warn that something similar could happen again. Meanwhile, other natural disasters occur on a more regular basis – floods, drought, disease, volcanic eruptions, and fires, for instance – all of which may lead to the decline of particular species and possibly their eventual disappearance.

Throughout the pages that follow, we take a look at the many and varied reasons why extinction sometimes occurs and trace the involvement of human beings in the demise of many lost species, usually through sheer greed and even complete carelessness on a great number of occasions.

DIRECT HIT
The chances of asteroids hitting Earth are remote, but it did happen 65 million years ago, causing many life forms to disappear forever.

CHAIN REACTIONS
For want of water, rivers and lakes will dry up, and fish will die. Plants will also wither, leaving little for plant-eaters to eat. Meat-eaters will suffer, too. Long periods of drought can bring devastation in their wake.

WELCOME TO THE WORLD!
While so many creatures have become extinct, fortunately, a number have reappeared when they were thought to have died out. Some have even been discovered for the first time. One of them is the okapi, seen here nuzzling her newborn calf.

Did the timber industry really have to destroy so much forest in the southeastern United States, with the result that the ivory-billed woodpecker's natural habitat has completely disappeared?

Why were so many extinct species of wolves once the victims of vicious poisoning campaigns? Did we human beings seriously need so much caribou meat and leather that the last surviving eastern elk – a most magnificent beast – was slaughtered in 1877? Must we continue to pollute our waters to such an extent that rare sealife is adversely affected? As you read on, decide for yourself whether the future looks bleak, or whether we can combine forces at a global level to save the world's endangered species.

STATE PROTECTION
The cougar *above* is now fully protected by law in parts of Florida, such as the Everglades National Park, but it remains severely endangered.

A FIERY FINISH
The elusive West Indian muskrat *below* became extinct as the result of the eruption of volcanic Mt. Pelée on the island of Martinique in 1902.

ASTEROIDS

This planet has never known such a catastrophe. Everywhere, the ground shook, there were violent volcanic eruptions, and clouds of poisonous ash spilled out into the atmosphere as a massive asteroid hit Earth. It was the start of the so-called Great Dying.

As far back as 251 million years ago, a seven-and-a-half-mile-wide object on a journey from outer space suddenly hit our planet at the incredible speed of 300,000 miles per hour. The resulting impact was so forceful that scientists estimate the cataclysmic event wiped out well over 90 percent of all existing life.

DEATH OF THE DINOSAURS
When an asteroid hit Earth 65 million years ago, tremendous clouds of dust blocked out sunlight for years on end and brought about the demise of the dinosaurs.

FUTURE SHOCK
Scientists have warned that an asteroid could hit our planet again at any time. The effect on animal and human life would depend on its size and the force of the impact.

8

FROM OUTER SPACE

Craters like the one *above* in Mexico provide evidence that asteroids from deep in outer space have hit our planet at various times, to devastating effect.

THE EVIDENCE

But what proof do scientists have that this really happened all that time ago? In Japan, China, and Hungary, where 250-million-year-old rocks have become exposed, scientists found tiny, spherical molecules called buckyballs. They occur in geological sediments at the boundary between the Permian era and the Triassic period, and inside them are atoms of the gases helium and argon that are unlike those normally found on Earth. They must have come from outer space, traveling here inside the enormous asteroid.

Asteroids are huge chunks of rock and miniature planets left over from when the larger planets formed, and exist in a belt around the Sun between Jupiter and Mars.

There are millions of asteroids, and sometimes they crash into each other and come hurtling out of orbit toward Earth. This is what also happened 65 million years ago, when the dinosaurs and other creatures became extinct at the end of Cretaceous times after an asteroid hit the coast of Mexico, causing fires, earthquakes, and giant tidal waves. It is also what some scientists think occurred far more recently, in 1908, at Tunguska, Siberia.

Whole forests were felled by the impact, while for over 100 miles everything was burned to a cinder. Yet, mysteriously, there was no crater to be seen. Many plants and animals exclusive to the Tunguska forest must have disappeared as a result of this cosmic accident. But meanwhile, the United States counted itself lucky. If the incident had occurred thirteen hours later, chances are New York would have been totally destroyed.

TAKING ACTION

Asteroid strikes are rare; but whenever they happen, the effects are truly devastating. However, what is most frightening is that they can occur with very little warning so that there is no time to move whole populations of humans and animals to safety. In any event, the impact of a very large asteroid could destroy our world completely. The odds of an asteroid hitting Earth in your lifetime stand at 20,000 to one. Nevertheless, astronomers and space scientists are currently working to develop ways of deflecting such cosmic debris.

ICE AGES

There have been several periods during Earth's long history when some seas froze, when there were huge snowfalls, and when ice covering the North Pole expanded southward. What caused these great chills, and how did they affect the planet's plants and animals?

FROZEN OVER
About one-tenth of the Earth is covered by ice today. But for much of our planet's history there was three times as much, as shown on the prehistoric world map, *above*.

THE ULTIMATE PREDATOR
It may not have been the severe cold that finally killed off many creatures of the Ice Ages but the human hunter.

The world's climate has frequently gone through great changes. Sometimes overall conditions were warmer, sometimes much colder. Scientists even know there must have been one Ice Age around 440 million years ago and another approximately 290 million years ago. In more recent Pleistocene times (which lasted from 2 million to 10,000 years ago) there are also thought to have been at least seven such Ice Ages.

Debate continues as to what causes an Ice Age. But according to one theory, developed by the Serbian physicist Milutin Milankovitch in 1913, drastic climatic change occurs in a cycle about every 22,000 years, when alteration in the Earth's tilt affects the amount of sunlight reaching polar regions and also the severity and duration of winter.

As for the effect of past glaciations (the Ice Ages) on animal life, over a huge span of time and as food became increasingly scarce, some adapted by becoming woollier and also smaller, since a decrease in their body size meant they could get by even when consuming far less.

TURNED TO ICE
A glacier forms from unmelted snow. Lower layers become squeezed together and turn to ice, which may slowly flow downhill. Upper layers are not squeezed but crack and shatter.

But during the Ice Ages there were also periods, known as interglacials, when it grew warmer before becoming cold again. During very harsh conditions some northern animals migrated as far south as they could, and others hibernated in caves. With spring the covering of ice and snow thinned, and heavier creatures frequently fell through to their deaths. Their bodies, though, remained frozen and in perfect condition over thousands of years. It is even said that meat from

Fact file

● Even during the numerous Ice Ages there were parts of the world near the equator that remained warm.

● During Precambrian times, which span about seven-eighths of our planet's history, there were at least four great Ice Ages.

● Some animals, such as lions and bears, took to living in caves during the Ice Ages.

● Prehistoric woolly rhinos and mammoths grew thick coats to keep them warm in freezing conditions.

● Scientists glean information about the temperatures of prehistoric times by studying the fossilized remains of animals, insects such as beetles, and also pollen from plants and trees of the past.

mammoth carcasses found in the permafrost was served at a 19th-century dinner attended by scientists in Russia!

ON FROZEN SOIL
During the Ice Ages much of the world resembled today's Arctic tundra, *right*, yet the frozen landscape still supported a number of different mammals.

BLOSSOMING SURVIVORS
The blue gentian flowers, *left*, are an example of mountain plants that are relics of the Ice Ages, during which they survived at high altitudes.

DROUGHT

Some plants and animals have adapted well to desert conditions. Camels store water and fat in their humps and the rose of Jericho will go dormant, reviving miraculously when it rains. But in the long term, without any water at all Earth would become a dead planet.

According to legend, the wise biblical King Solomon was once asked by the beautiful Queen of Sheba what he thought was most valuable in her country, Ethiopia. She had expected an immediate answer – rubies, sapphires, or gold, perhaps.

However, the king delayed a response and instead ordered a lavish banquet to be prepared, including arrays of salted meats and the sweetest of wines. The queen was to be his honored guest.

That night, after the meal the queen awoke from a deep sleep and felt her throat was parched. It was all she could do to drag herself out of bed to fetch water.

King Solomon, it is said, had hidden nearby; and as the queen went to fill her goblet, he asked the very same question she herself had posed just a few hours previously. The queen now answered that the most precious thing in a dry land is surely water.

Ethiopia, the Sudan, and Chad, all in Africa, are currently in a period of terrible drought, as are several other parts of the world. Indeed, the Sudan is known to have had a dramatic decline in rainfall since 1960, and it is getting worse all the time. What, though, is causing this? Meteorologists (scientists studying weather patterns) think weak winds in Europe, which can prevent rainfall from reaching parts of Africa, may be to blame. Meanwhile, winter rainfall in Mediterranean regions of Europe has been on the increase.

But nature can still pull a few surprises out of the hat; so perhaps, in time, these badly affected African countries may once more be lush enough to support a wide variety of plants and animals. Such wonders have happened elsewhere.

GONE FISHING
The Utah Lake sculpin shown in this illustration were lost to anglers when they became extinct as the result of drought in 1936.

DRY AS A BONE
In the long term lack of rain would totally wipe out life on Earth. But even short spells of drought can spell disaster for many creatures, as shown in this photograph taken in southern Africa.

Australia's Lake Eyre, for example, was long one of the planet's most inhospitable places, having completely dried out due to lack of water and extreme heat. As a result, this part of the Outback was without life for about 200 years.

Now, however, thanks to unexpected heavy rainfall, this inland sea is once more home to many birds, fish, and insects, as well as plants.

The arum lily, for example, had lain dormant for years but started to blossom when the monsoon rains came; and as shrimp hatched out, fish washed down by newly flowing rivers could feed on them. Pelicans also soon returned in their hundreds to feast on herring. The downside, however, is that no one knows how long this superb reawakening of life in a previously arid region will last. Prolonged drought could set in yet again. In the end extensive irrigation programs may be the only way to ensure the survival of many species, including human beings, living in regions where it fails to rain.

A DESERT DEATH
The gemsbok, *right*, usually fleet of foot and very alert, has collapsed through lack of water.

VOLCANIC ACTIVITY

Although some scientists believe life on this planet first came about as a result of volcanic eruptions from deep within the Earth's core, over millions of years torrents of boiling lava and ash have destroyed both plants and animals.

As you read this, at least one of the world's 550 active volcanoes is likely to be erupting. The most disastrous eruption occurred in 1815, when 92,000 people and countless animals lost their lives.

LAST GOODBYE
A West Indian muskrat looks on as Mt. Pelée erupts and destroys its natural habitat.

BOILING OVER
On the Mediterranean island of Sicily Mount Etna erupts at frequent intervals. Here you can see lava streaming from this volcano. Its temperature is an incredible 1,000 degrees Celsius.

But what about specific species known to have become extinct due to such eruptions? Once hunted and eaten by people living on the Caribbean island of Martinique, a species of muskrat with the name Megalomys demarestii (<u>MEG</u>-AL-<u>OM</u>-ISS <u>DEM</u>-AR-<u>EST</u>-EE-EE) has not been seen since 1902. It disappeared completely after a massive volcanic eruption, just as many other creatures have done in other parts of the world over time.

Ten million years ago in Nebraska, for instance, dense clouds of poisonous dust were blown for thousands of miles after a similar disaster.

It caused whole herds of prehistoric deer and three-toed horses, as well as many other species, to suffocate. They would have endured a slow and agonizing death.

WELL PRESERVED

But there is a brighter side to the story, at least from a scientific point of view. Many such remains were discovered near a former waterhole in 1979, and the fossils were painstakingly removed from the site by paleontologists who, millions of years later, still had to protect themselves from the remaining dust.

Some complete skeletons were unearthed and had been extraordinarily well preserved due to this thick, protective blanket of volcanic ash. Fossil grass seeds were even found in a rhino's throat cavity, and the stomachs of certain extinct wading birds still contained meals of mice and lizards. The natural disaster caused horrific loss of animal and plant life at the time, but it has at least left us with valuable fossil evidence.

Fact file

- The volcano destroying gigantic rhinos, camels, and three-toed horses among many other prehistoric animals in Nebraska ten million years ago probably erupted over 600 miles away in New Mexico.

- When Mount Pinatubo in the Philippines erupted in 1991, within three weeks a girdle of thin dust circled the entire globe, causing sunlight to be deflected and a slight cooling of temperatures.

- In spite of the damage it causes, a volcano has a valuable contribution to make. There are important minerals in lava flow that help make soil fertile. Their energy may also one day be widely harnessed, as it already is in volcanic Iceland, to provide a nonpolluting source of power.

CHOKED TO DEATH
The aftermath can be just as catastrophic as moment of eruption, as this photograph of a valley near the Pinatubo volcano in the Philippines, covered in volcanic ash, clearly shows. Much of the local wildlife probably choked to death after inhaling the dust.

EARTHQUAKES

It is hardly any wonder people have long been wary of earthquakes. Worldwide about 500,000 earthquakes occur every year; and though most are so small that they are not felt by us, some cause not only devastating damage but tremendous loss of life.

The world's worst recorded earthquake occurred in 1557 in central China. Here, it is estimated that as many as 830,000 people who were living in caves may have lost their lives. More recently, too, in 1976, approximately 250,000 Chinese citizens perished when another mighty earthquake struck.

What, though, causes an earthquake? And why is it that some parts of the world are far more vulnerable than others? Sudden violent shaking of the ground occurs when part of the Earth's normally rigid and cool outer shell changes position as part of a phenomenon known as plate tectonics. This is even known to happen on the surface of the Moon.

Shock waves are sent out, and they are sometimes so powerful that they open up great cracks in the ground to disastrous effect.

Seismologists – scientists who study, measure, and try to forecast earthquakes – know that they mainly take place along two great earthquake belts girdling the planet. One of them encircles the Pacific Ocean and runs along the coasts of North and South America and through some of the islands of Asia. California and Nevada have frequently felt the effects.

The second main earthquake belt runs between Europe and North Africa and includes other parts of Asia, but it is not nearly so active.

UNKNOWN QUANTITY
On average, 10,000 people currently die each year as a result of significant earthquakes. Devastation is obviously worst in cities, as depicted here. But no one can hazard a guess as to how much wildlife is lost forever when this greatly feared phenomenon occurs.

CRACKING UP
The San Andreas fault lies along the west coast of California. Here, two great sections of the Earth's crust, known as plates, are trying to slide past each other, as shown in the diagram *below*. This triggers frequent earthquakes.

NO ONE'S FAULT
In 1906, and again in 1989, parts of San Francisco were destroyed as the result of mighty earthquakes and had to be rebuilt. The aerial photograph *left* clearly shows California's San Andreas fault as a deep crack. No one knows when a similar disaster may occur again.

Fact file

- The outermost layer of the Earth is known as the lithosphere. It includes the planet's cool crust and, below it, the partly melted, hot rocks of a layer known as the upper mantle, extending down to about 400 miles from the surface.

- Below the upper mantle lies the far deeper lower mantle, which is solid and continues for about 1,400 miles.

- Under the lower mantle is the Earth's outer core. It is liquid nickel and iron.

- Next comes the inner core, which is the center of the Earth. It is solid and stays that way, even though its temperature is well over 4,000 degrees Celsius because of the pressure from above.

ANIMAL REACTIONS
If there was a sure way to predict a large earthquake, maybe it would be possible to escape in time. In the attempt to give such warnings, not only do seismologists consult their complex equipment, they also now listen to reports of unusual animal behavior. Dogs, horses, birds, and even fish often act in a peculiar way several days before an earthquake. The widely accepted explanation is that they can sense small foreshocks before the catastrophic event, but some scientists suspect they may be responding to the gradual release of certain gases.

Bad earthquakes are, of course, very harmful to the entire ecosystem. Many animals and plants alike, some possibly endangered, may be wiped out by resulting fires, while those that do survive are sure to be affected by damage to the soil. Indeed, nothing may grow for several years because important organic material has been destroyed. Property can be rebuilt over time following an earthquake. But lost species may never be replaced.

TAKING MEASURES
Seismographs, like the one shown *right*, are used throughout the world's earthquake belts to produce readings that both predict to some extent and measure the force of an earthquake.

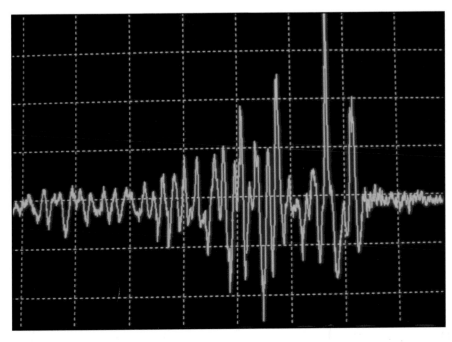

DEADLY DISEASES

A great many factors continue to contribute to the deaths of many of the world's species. But we tend to forget that animals and plants can fall victim to epidemics and fatal illnesses, just as humans do, in spite of tremendous advances in medical treatment.

The white Bengal tiger is, alas, severely endangered. Indeed, fewer than 130 are now thought to remain in a wildlife park in India. Thirteen of that country's national animal died in the year 2000 from a nasty disease spread by the tsetse fly. A true tragedy had struck. What was more, a rare type of Indian deer living in the same park also succumbed to the disease, which seemed not to affect humans.

KILLER VIRUSES
Many illnesses for which there are no known cures as yet spread like wildfire and may affect both humans and animals. Among them is the AIDS virus, shown *below* under the microscope.

But diseases can sometimes spread so rapidly that they will virtually wipe out even a very numerous species. The severe epidemic of myxomatosis (MIX-OH-MAT-OH-SIS) that arrived in Great Britain in 1954, for example, killed almost all wild rabbits. It also had a marked chain effect. Grasslands, for instance, then grew so strongly that small, flowering herbs went into rapid decline. Animals such as weasels were affected, too, by the loss of rabbits, their staple diet.

BUNNY BLIGHT
As the result of an epidemic of the disease known as myxomotosis, which affects rabbits, the entire ecosystem of Great Britain was disturbed, and the effects are still felt today.

Many years later rabbits are once more a familiar sight in the British countryside: but disease has taken its toll, and the ecological balance has changed, perhaps forever.

ACROSS THE SPECIES
Some diseases are also known to pass from domestic animals to those in the wild. In Tanzania's foremost national park, for instance, the grazing of domestic animals in the vicinity of wildebeest resulted in the transfer of foot-and-mouth disease, and as a result thousands of magnificent beasts went to their death. Dogs in Africa are also known to have spread distemper and rabies to lions.

But many domestic animals are in peril, too. According to an organization monitoring information from 170 countries, on average every week two breeds are lost, and one-third are now thought to be seriously at risk. By 2020 as many as 2,000 different breeds could have become extinct.

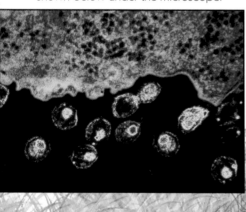

SAVING RARE DOMESTIC BREEDS
Endangered domestic breeds were isolated and infected farm animals slaughtered when foot-and-mouth disease broke out in Great Britain in 2001.

Among them are breeds of cattle, sheep, goats, horses, pigs, yaks, chickens, geese, ducks, turkeys, and the ostriches that are now farmed for food.

Humans can also catch diseases from animals, of course. Indeed, though no one knows for sure, some scientists suspect that the AIDS virus may originally have passed to us from African monkeys.

Not only in southern Africa but all around the world the number of people known to be at risk of developing full-blown AIDS is on the increase among both men and women. Clearly we need to take all possible preventive measures and find a cure. If not, and AIDS spreads further, might it lead to the extinction of our own species, *Homo sapiens*?

Fact file

● Mysteriously, a frog-killing fungus turned up almost simultaneously in places as far apart as Australia, Panama, and the United States. Scientists now think that by an unfortunate accident they may themselves have spread it as a result of visiting different environments to study endangered amphibians.

● The manatee is one of the world's most endangered species. So it is all the more alarming that some of the captive population have been found with an infection causing skin growths that may develop to such an extent that they interfere with feeding and sight. Breathing may also be affected, and there is a risk that the growths could become malignant.

LOST ISLAND LIFE

A great many birds and plants have become extinct on the islands of Hawaii since the great British explorer Captain Cook discovered this archipelago in 1778. What is more, a large number of its native species are endangered today. Why should this be?

The most isolated island group in the world, Hawaii must have been a virtual paradise on Earth for millions of years. As far as is known, there were never any large mammals on the archipelago to disturb its infinite variety of colorful birds and plants, but that all changed once humans came to the region.

The first to arrive, well over 1,000 years ago, were the Polynesians. What greeted them was a lush environment that previously had been unexposed to outside influences. Later settlers brought livestock from Europe. They also cut down forests to provide land for grazing and for growing crops. And so, increasingly, many of the islands' unique plants and animals were to become extinct.

A PIG OF A PROBLEM

Among the creatures most at blame, both historically and even today, are wild pigs. In all, there are probably as many as 100,000 still wandering the islands, uprooting the native plants as they feed on roots and shoots, all the while spreading in their droppings the seeds of introduced plants that continue to gain a stranglehold on the imperiled native vegetation.

Goats and mongooses came to the islands along with settlers, and their presence had a marked effect on wildlife, too. Indeed, as many as 2,000 species of birds and plants once exclusive to the islands of Hawaii are thought to have been lost over the last eight centuries as the region's human population flourished.

Due to habitat destruction, several species of the islands' honeycreepers and honeyeaters have not been seen for more than a hundred years. Until the mid-19th century some were even taken in their hundreds of thousands by descendants of the original Polynesian settlers so their vibrant feathers could be used to decorate elaborate traditional cloaks.

Avian malaria also killed off some of the archipelago's birds. Cats, rats, and dogs took their toll, too, while for no known reason the introduction of cattle seems to have affected Hawaii's bird life.

IN A STATE

Hawaii is sometimes said to be America's most adversely affected state when it comes to endangered species. Numbers of its official bird, the nene, have even gone into severe decline. However, much is being done by dedicated conservationists to remedy the situation. Rare plants are carefully cultivated out of harm's way, while special breeding programs for endangered birds have been introduced. How wonderful if we could also save the 5,000 Hawaiian species that scientists estimate remain undiscovered!

YESTERDAY ON HAWAII

In this landscape of long ago you will find several of the missing species of the Hawaiian Islands. Use the key that follows to identify them.
A very long-billed honeycreeper (1); a crested variety (2); and the orange-black damselfly (3) are all very rare today. The long-legged Maui owl (4) is extinct, as is the flightless ibis (5.) We also know that the flightless, tortoise-jawed moa (6) existed on these islands well over 1,000 years ago due to the discovery of its fossilized remains. Few of the exquisite species of flowering hibiscus (7) and Hawaiian black-and-white stilt (8) remain, and the parrotlike Kona grosbeak (9) was last sighted in 1894.

Fact file

- The Hawaiian woodpecker is dying out due to deforestation.

- The *po'ouli* (<u>POH</u>-OO-LEE), probably the most endangered bird in the whole world and only discovered in 1973, is thought to have died out because it was preyed on by rats.

- Plants sometimes die out because the creatures that previously played an important role in their pollination have become extinct, too. On Hawaii, for instance, certain flowering trees vanished due to the disappearance of certain species of nectar-feeding honeycreeper birds. The long-beaked honeycreepers had played much the same role as bees do in the pollination of other plants.

FIRES

Flames are, of course, destructive and have definitely contributed to the extinction of several species of plants and animals. But there are plants that actually depend on fires at a certain time of the year and at a particular temperature for their seeds to sprout .

Hard as it may be to believe, certain forest trees have developed a very good relationship with fire. Indeed, fires can actually save some types of trees from dying out.

What is important, however, is that such fires occur at regular intervals. Take the splendid ponderosa pines of western North America, for example. They were subjected to dreadful burning in 1994 as the result of a huge forest fire. But, ironically, it occurred as a result of overprotection.

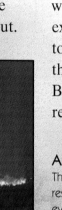

ALL ABLAZE
The fierce fire *left* occurred at a game reserve in South Africa. No one will ever know how many rare species of animals, insects, and plants were lost as a result of it.

ISLAND INFERNOS
Not only has destruction of rain forest on the island of Madagascar for farmland resulted in loss of habitat for so much of this island's wildlife, associated fires have killed off many rare species, too.

Over many years efforts had been made to suppress any small fires that arose, and so deadwood piled up on forest floors while small groves of trees soon started to sprout in spaces between the older, more established trees. Lack of rainfall, wind, and lightning then combined to produce a dreadful, towering inferno.

BURNED TO DEATH
The broad-faced potoroos shown in this illustration finally became extinct in parts of Australia in 1908. Their demise was partly due to bush fires.

BLESSING AND A CURSE

Scientific research has shown that almost every sort of ecosystem on the planet actually requires fire to clear it of waste if it is to survive. Fire can also help turn dead matter into nutrients for plants and will promote sprouting of some types of seeds. There are even birds that only thrive because of fires that prevent their forest habitat from becoming overgrown. The careful management of fire has therefore become a type of science in its own right. Prairies are set alight each spring in Kansas but well-controlled, they will only last a few days. Then just one month later ranched cattle will be enjoying the fresh grass that springs up.

EARLY START
In Australia today, instead of risking bush fires later in the dry season when they are likely to be fiercer, some are started early to avoid unnecessary destruction.

But 50,000 years ago no one had any idea why and how to control fire. Some scientists even think that early humans in Australia unintentionally caused the country's large animals to become extinct through uncontrolled fires that not only burned lots of species to death but also destroyed their food supplies so that starvation set in.

Fact file

● The Apache Indian tribe traditionally regards fire as sacred. Indeed, they believe it provides them not only with warmth but also, indirectly, with food. Long before scientists first realized fire was vital to forests and grasslands, these Indians had some knowledge of the part it can play in seed germination.

● When forest fires burn at a temperature far too high for the soil so that it becomes completely baked, rain water can no longer be absorbed, and it may take many years or possibly centuries for a full recovery of plant life.

● Some fires are started intentionally by foresters to create room for new seedlings to grow.

HUNTING

Mankind has been a hunter right from the time we first evolved. As a result, countless creatures have become extinct, often dying at our hands in the most horrible ways. Regrettably, today, too, the chase continues.

RAIN FOREST RARITY

The male mandrill is among the most spectacular of all monkeys with its very colorful face and hind quarters. But in spite of legislation, it is still hunted in the wild and has become one of the rarest monkeys in the rain forests of Africa.

Sought and killed primarily for its skin rather than its flesh, the blue antelope or *blaauwbok* (<u>BLOHW</u>-BOK) – its name in the Afrikaans language – of South Africa was first described in 1731. At that time it was already rare and, as far as we know, had never been found in large numbers. But greedy hunters carried on regardless, continuing to kill this species until, 69 years later, it was gone.

IN PREHISTORIC TIMES
Early human beings were mainly meat-eaters, and the demise of some extinct beasts, such as the aurochs, is certainly at least partly due to predation by our ancestors.

A species of deer known as Dawson's caribou, meanwhile, was once found only on Graham Island off British Columbia, Canada. During the 19th century immigrants hunted them for their long, thick winter coats and also ate their flesh. Finally, the last three adults were shot in 1908, but a baby got away. It was the end of the line.

Similarly, American bison once roamed the great plains in their millions, where Native Americans hunted them not only for their meat but also for their hides. But wholesale slaughter soon began with the arrival of Europeans.

WHALE WARNING
Many governments now have legislation to control whaling, but the problem remains within international waters. Several species are severely endangered.

Buffalo Bill is even said to have killed over 4,250 of the bison in just 18 months to provide sufficient food for the men building railroads across the continent at the time. Some historians suspect that a corrupt government also had these animals killed specifically to ruin the Plains Indians' economy. Soon the bison were a dying breed. In 1860 there were only about 850 left. But fortunately there is a happy ending to their story. Thanks to a successful conservation program there are now thought to be as many as 350,000 on ranches and in state parks throughout North America, though this is of course only a fraction of their original numbers.

Fact file

- The Sumatran species is one of the rarest of all the rhinos, but it is still hunted for its horns and hide. The current price for two pounds of rhino horn, thought by some people to have medicinal properties, although this has not been proven, is about $60,000 in the Far East.

- Arabian oryxes – once hunted for their meat, horns, and hide, and now highly endangered – were once chased by hunters in jeeps until the animals dropped from sheer exhaustion. Their throats would then be cut.

- Sometimes animals become endangered as the result of being caught in traps set for other animals. The giant panda that inhabits pine forests in China is one such victim.

A SORRY END
The taking of crocodiles may be banned in some places, but the prices their skins will fetch are so high that it is hard to stop the activity of poachers, such as those who have so cruelly pierced this specimen with a spear in Mato Grosso, Brazil.

SAD SOUVENIRS
Cruelly killed to satisfy the tourist trade, the three turtle shells displayed, *right*, in a market on the island of Martinique in the West Indies will doubtless fetch a good price, but the species is unnecessarily depleted in this way.

DESTRUCTION OF HABITAT

Change an animal or plant's natural environment, and chances are you will endanger that species or even bring it to the brink of extinction. Unfortunately, the loss of so much of our planet's plants and animals shows that we humans learned this lesson far too late.

LOST LYNXES
One of the Europe's rarest mammals, the Spanish lynx is rarely seen today. Among several factors responsible for its decline is the destruction of its favored woodland habitat, as depicted in the illustration *below*.

FELLED FOR FARMING
In newly cleared Madagascan rain forest, farmers can be seen planting their crops. No one can hazard a guess as to how many of the island's species have been put at risk or will die out as a result.

The plants and animals of Africa, Asia, and South America have been very hard hit by the clearance of forests. Indeed, on all three continents trees have been widely felled to provide land for subsistance farming or for wood that is used for cooking, heating, or as fuel for small industries such as brick-making and tobacco-curing. Logging and the removal of other vegetation often means that the soil loses the ability to hold water, becoming arid and stripped of vital nutrients. Local wildlife therefore moves on or becomes severely endangered. That is exactly what has happened in Tanzania, Africa, for example, where antelopes such as eland and kudu have now died out, and where birds such as the fish eagle are no longer to be seen.

BARKING UP THE WRONG TREE
The farmer seen felling a tree in the rain forest of Borneo to clear an area for planting crops risks endangering several rare jungle species.

NUCLEAR DISASTER

But the devastation of a habitat can sometimes happen as the result of unfortunate accidents, such as the worst nuclear plant explosion in history that occurred in 1986 at Chernobyl, Belarus. Many local children developed cancer and other serious illnesses as a result of the disaster, and a reserve was set up to monitor the effects of the radioactivity on native plants and wildlife. Conservationists naturally hope it will be the only radioactive nature reserve ever to exist on our planet.

At first, the press reported terrible mutations. Foals and calves were born without eyes, and there was even a rumor about a colt with eight legs. Not only had the entire ecosystem of the region been destroyed, but the effect had spread far afield to other countries. As many as 2,700 reindeer had to be slaughtered in Sweden, for example, because of the high level of radiation found in their bodies.

Yet 25 years later there is hope. Abnormalities are few; much forest has been replanted; and bears, deer, foxes, wolves, lynx, herons, and swans are among those creatures now to be found within less-contaminated areas of the 60-mile danger zone.

Fact file

- The exploitation of oil reserves in the tundra or polar deserts of the world has affected the soil in those regions, while overland pipelines have disrupted the migration routes of local species.

- In the last 200 years the world has probably lost about half of its tropical forests.

- The rain forests, which continue to be vulnerable to the effects of logging, are thought to be home to about 40% of all the world's plant and animal species.

- The drastic reduction in the orangutan population of Borneo, Indonesia, is a prime example of how destruction of an animal's natural rain forest habitat can bring it to near extinction.

But as wild animals return and appear to be thriving, scientists have spotted a number of changes in their genetic makeup. So only in the long term can we assess the true impact of such a disaster.

TRUE PROGRESS?
Surely we are going backward with conservation when roads are built through an endangered species' natural habitat, as in the Malaysian forest *below*?

FASHION VICTIMS

When people wear very smart clothes, according to an old expression they are "dressed to kill." Those who choose to wear furs, however, are sometimes said to kill to dress. Many people blame the fashion industry for endangering certain rare species.

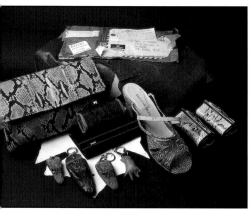

CROCODILE WALK
Crocodile shoes were once thought the height of elegance, and millions of these beasts were killed and skinned to make such accessories, as well as purses.

Claims are sometimes made that the fur industry is in severe decline due to general public recognition that the killing of animals for this purpose is not only cruel but endangers rare species even further. However, recent statistics could not be more alarming. According to a current estimate, as many as 10 million animals are still trapped in the wild each year for their fur, which is then supplied to the fashion industry. What is more, for every one of those animals killed in this way, other creatures not specifically targeted for their pelts – squirrels, dogs, cats, and birds of prey, for example – become caught in the baited snares.

Some animals such as mink and foxes, meanwhile, are raised on farms and when mature are killed by such horrific methods as gas, neck-breaking, electrocution, or injection. They lose their beautiful coats merely so that garments can be made for the fashion industry.

Many species eventually died out altogether after being taken in huge numbers for their skins. Among them were the blue antelope of southern Africa, Grey's wallaby, which lived in Australia, Dawson's caribou of Canada, and the West Indian monk seal.

Today, too, several species are highly endangered for the very same reason.

Indeed, the slow loris of Southeast Asia, Africa's cheetah, leopards, the tiger, and a number of snakes are growing increasingly rare.

FOR AND AGAINST

But there are those who maintain the fur industry, if carefully managed, will actually bring benefits to other forms of wildlife. Fur-bearing animals often give birth to more young than their natural habitat can support, they argue, so survival of these species should not be threatened. They also state that the fur trade contributes financially to wildlife research projects, and that it is in fact committed to the cause of conservation.

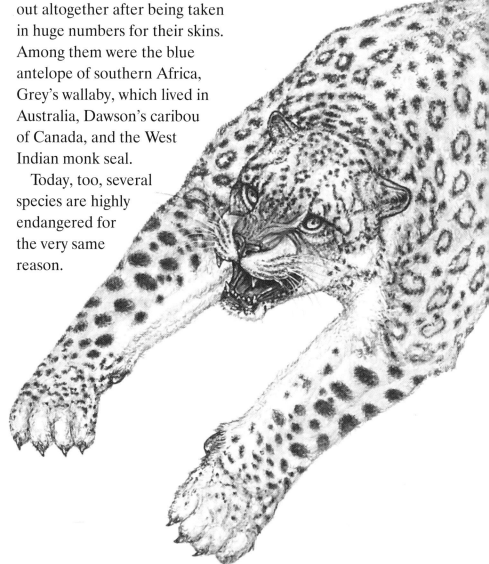

FAKING IT

Manufacturers can now produce such excellent fake furs that they are hard to tell apart from the genuine article. Conservationists are therefore baffled as to why some of our rarest species are still killed for their skins.

PRECIOUS FEW

The snow leopard, or ounce, is becoming rarer with each passing year since its pelt, *left*, is among the most highly prized in the world.

But it is not only the desire for fur that feeds the fashion industry. Crocodile and alligator skins are also sought and made into shoes, purses, and other items. Indeed, those working with the tanning of leather derived from these reptiles say that demand still exceeds supply. Many species of crocodiles are protected by law, but poachers in Africa and South America particularly are always on the lookout for these reptiles because of the huge profits to be made.

Increasingly, however, large commercial companies and multinational organizations, in spite of a reputation to the contrary, are trying to contribute to conservation of endangered species, and they sometimes do it in highly innovative ways. Even so, when it comes to fashion, there are those who stand in their way. A major toy-maker, for example, once promised to give one dollar from the sale of each of its trendy toy seals to the Humane Society of the United States.

But seal hunters resented these marketing methods and so arranged for the company to be swamped with so much correspondence about the matter that it had to withdraw its pledge, although finally another toy firm went ahead with something similar. The long war against the cruel killing of endangered species clearly still has to be won.

IGNORING THE LAW

The photograph *right* shows poachers killing a jaguar for its pelt. Despite legislation, these handsome spotted cats are still hunted and fetch a high price.

Polluted Waters

The dumping of chemicals and toxic waste into seas and rivers wreaks havoc with wildlife. Sometimes, too, appalling accidents occur – oil spills, for example. But there is increasing evidence that an extraordinary natural occurrence sometimes also takes its toll.

TROUBLED WATERS
Slicks like the one *above* may occur if a tanker runs aground, spilling large quantities of oil into the sea. As a result, birds, fish, and other forms of marine life will become severely poisoned.

One morning in 1947 the residents of Venice, Florida, awoke to find thousands of dead fish lying along the beaches. In 1984 a herd of cows in Montana collapsed and died only a few minutes after drinking from a pool. In 1998, 400 sealions tried to drag themselves ashore around Monterey Bay, California. They were sick, observers remarked. Some staggered; others were comatose.

When zoologists examined those that died, they were astonished to find in their stomachs traces of a highly poisonous acid occurring in some types of algal bloom.

A STICKY END
This unfortunate cormorant is sticky with oil from a major spill. Thousands of birds can be affected by such accidents; and even though rescuers try to clean them up, most will probably die.

But what exactly are algal blooms? And are they all so toxic? Strange as it may seem in the light of the reaction of these sealions, seacows, and many fish, most forms of algal blooms are highly beneficial. They are in fact at the root of the entire marine food chain. But some are not so friendly. They include microscopic organisms that are predatory and capable of killing a fish with the emission of a cocktail of lethal chemicals.

RED TIDES

Reports of such occurrences have been recorded since the mid-19th century and are currently on the increase in many parts of the world. One drop of water may contain millions of these miniature killers. So when did they first strike? They may have existed for many millions of years; and researchers have even suggested that one of the biblical plagues – seas full of blood – may actually have been an incidence of what is known as a red tide, since some species of these toxic organisms will cause a brownish-red sheen on the water's surface.

Some red tides have been known to cover several hundred square miles of ocean, and the difficulty is that no one as yet has found a way of predicting when, where, or for how long they will occur. Sometimes they last for a few months in one location, but it can be for more than a whole year.

BAD TIDINGS
Oil spills have contributed to the decline of the puffin on Atlantic islands, as have reduced fish supplies due to the effect of poisonous red tides.

The causative organisms lie dormant most of the time, but suddenly a not fully understood trigger turns them toxic.

But it is not only fish and animals that can be affected by these toxins. Birds such as cormorants and pelicans have died after eating infected anchovies, and human beings are also at risk.

Oysters, mussels, and clams, for instance, readily become contaminated; and when humans eat them, they too can suffer dreadful consequences. It could even be that certain ancient religious dietary laws prohibiting the eating of such shellfish arose from experience of such poisoning.

What is worrying, too, is that as a result of pollution of the oceans through the wholesale dumping of phosphates and other waste products containing nutrients, these harmful organisms could be getting the very substances they need to promote their growth.

A STICKY MOMENT
The photograph *below* shows a struggling seabird being tube-fed by one conservationist while another holds it still. The poor creature had become covered in oil from a leaking tanker, but was rescued and taken to a sanctuary.

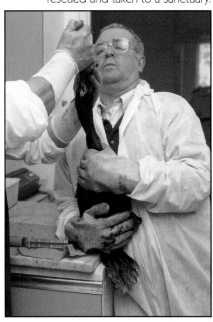

ACID RAIN

When rain falls today, it does not usually consist of pure water but contains various substances, some of which can have a very harmful effect on the soil, on trees and plants, and on other living things. What causes this, and is there anything that can be done to prevent it?

DIATOM DISCOVERIES
Scientists can study the level of acidity in lakes by examining microscopic algae, called diatoms, shown *above*. Changes usually relate to increased pollution.

When we light certain types of coal fires, when cars running on gas produce nasty fumes, and when factories belch out smoke, acid rain is formed as the chemicals emitted combine with moisture in the atmosphere and fall as rain or snow.

When this acid rain falls, it washes away important nutrients in the soil, such as calcium and magnesium, and prevents normal photosynthesis so that trees and plants may literally may starve to death. But the phenomenon is not just a recent one. In fact, scientists believe it has been going on since way before humans first appeared on Earth.

The mass extinction that occurred at the end of Cretaceous times, 65 million years ago, for instance, when an asteroid collided with our planet, is thought to have been due in part to the acid rain that fell over many years after poisonous substances were forced up into the air.

DEADWOOD
Experts think that approximately half the trees in several countries of the world have been damaged by the effects of acid rain either directly or through a reduction in their frost-hardiness.

Acid rain has been described as a pollutant cocktail. Its direct effect is primarily on trees and plants, but wildlife is eventually affected by the loss of plants and so are our lakes and rivers.

Many of the world's rain forests and woodlands may have been saved from the axe in the attempt to preserve these wonderful natural habitats. But the effect of acid rain on these environments continues to provide very serious cause for concern in spite of efforts on the part of many countries to reduce harmful emissions of sulfuric and nitric acids.

In cities nitric oxides are discharged in car exhausts and then carried in the air and dispersed downwind before falling as acid rain perhaps as far as 3,000 miles away. This means that in North America, for example, acids from the United States could be carried to Canada and impoverish the soil there.

In woodlands, meanwhile, most conifers and deciduous trees rely on a fungus that lives on their roots. Between the tree and the fungus there is a sort of symbiosis. The tree obtains water and essential minerals from the fungus, and the fungus gets nourishment from the tree. However, if the there is too much nitrogen in the air, this breaks down when the waxy covering of a leaf dissolves, leaving cells open to infection, and roots begin to rot.

FUMING OVER FUMES
Conservationists rightly complain that exhaust causes untold damage to the environment and champion the development of less polluting energy.

TAKING THE BLAME

Acid rain falls on water, too, and affects the harvest of fish from rivers and lakes. Indeed, some of the water-courses in Europe and North America have lost all their fish in this way and no longer support much underwater life at all. Such pollution is also held responsible for the rise in Alzheimer's disease, a condition affecting human mental capacity, and the erosion of such ancient buildings as the Parthenon in Athens, Greece, which has seen more damage in the last 50 years due to pollution than it has since it was built 2,000 years ago. Conservationists have suggested various interim measures, but the only truly effective solution must be the prompt elimination of sulfur and nitric acid emissions. Cost should not be prohibitive when it comes to maintaining our natural heritage.

Fact file

- The main cause of acid rain is sulfur dioxide, a gas emitted by volcanoes, rotting vegetation, and the burning of fossil fuels such as coal and oil. Emissions of nitric oxide from power stations and exhaust fumes are also components of acid rain.

- When acid rain falls, trees may become severely damaged as toxins such as aluminum are released from the soil.

- Acid rain can also have an effect on the human population, causing respiratory problems.

- Acid rain is measured using a pH scale. The lower its pH reading, the more acidic a substance is. Pure water has a pH reading of 7.0. In 2001 acidic rain falling in the U.S. had a reading of about 4.3.

UP AND DOWN
Every day, in spite of warnings, choking smoke from industrial chimneys rises into the air but never totally disperses since the pollutants it contains fall to earth as acid rain.

CHANGES IN CLIMATE

Global warming has been described as a threat to all living things on Earth and the greatest environmental challenge of the 21st century. But what would be to blame if the predicted global increase in temperature did occur? And could anything be done to curtail it?

The prospect of the planet getting warmer might seem beneficial when you first start to think about it. There would be less demand for energy for heating, for example. But at the same time, there would be many losers. Many endangered species might even reach the brink of extinction due to an inability to adapt quickly enough.

Indeed, unless drastic measures are taken to slow down changes currently taking place in the world's climate, scientists working for the United Nations warned in October 2001 that sea levels could rise by as much as 300 feet over the next millennium, with the result that some land masses could be transformed into no more than a series of tiny islands.

Even a sustained increase of one degree Celsius could affect the viability of certain trees, so that whole forests might disappear, to be replaced by entirely new ecosystems. Equally, flooding of many of the world's habitats might occur, so that certain species die out locally.

Several factors are thought to be responsible for climatic change. One is the so-called greenhouse effect. Just as gardeners grow seedlings in the warm and well-protected environment of a greenhouse, so the Earth is surrounded by an invisible atmospheric shield.

ANOTHER GREAT FLOOD?
If icebergs like the one *above* melt due to global warming, sea levels could rise to a dangerous level, and the effect on plants and animals could be devastating.

This protective layer contains gases that help keep the planet warm. But through excessive burning of fossil fuels we are now feeding back into the atmosphere great quantities of these gases – carbon dioxide in particular – with global warming as the outcome. Results are already visible. In the United States, for example, the natural habitat of a number of butterflies has moved further north to cooler regions as a direct reaction to the increase in temperature.

The destruction of our rain forests has also had a part to play in the release of more carbon dioxide into the atmosphere than has been experienced on this planet for millions of years. Some scientists, meanwhile, have suggested that interplanetary dust and movement in our planet's orbit around the Sun have both regularly had an influence on the Earth's climate in 100,000-year cycles. But we will need to act quickly to stand a chance of reversing the current trend.

WORLDS OF SAND
Desertification – a change in the Earth's surface due to erosion and global warming so that previously productive land is converted to desert, as shown here – is a threat currently faced by several countries in Africa, Asia, Latin America, and the northern Mediterranean. It is even estimated that as much as one-quarter of the Earth's surface faces a similar risk.

MASS EXTINCTIONS

It is estimated that of all the animals and plants ever to have existed, only about one in a thousand survives today. Indeed, most of those species that have disappeared from our planet became extinct within 10 million years of evolving. But these life forms did not always die out gradually. Instead, some vanished as part of several mass extinctions that have occurred over the millennia. Why did this happen? And will it occur again?

Be prepared for some startling statistics. Incredible as it may seem, experts estimate our planet is currently losing forever three different species every single hour – or as many as 30,000 each year.

Five mass extinctions have occurred on our planet since life began, and scientists believe that right now we are in the middle of a sixth.

SAVING THE ANIMALS
Tales of a great flood occur in the myths of so many societies that it seems likely a deluge like the one recounted in the Old Testament, from which Noah is said to have rescued animal life by building an ark, did indeed occur.

A GREAT ENIGMA

No one knows why many creatures, like the great white shark *above*, which has existed for many millions of years but is now vulnerable, survived the planet's mass extinctions.

All previous mass extinctions are said to have been due to natural causes. The first, for instance, is thought by many paleontolgists to have been the result of global cooling. Volcanic eruptions on a worldwide scale, warmer temperatures, and cataclysmic collisions with extraterrestrial bodies, such as asteroids, are also cited. But the sixth extinction, some paleontologists say, is very different. This time we humans are at least partly to blame for what has been occurring.

According to this viewpoint, it all started about 100,000 years ago when our ancestors first began to spread from Africa to various other parts of the planet. As we moved, we destroyed many natural habitats.

HUGE LOSSES

Early humans also hunted large plant-eaters on a grand scale, and such overkill may in turn have brought about the deaths of other, smaller species. About 10,000 years ago in North America, for example, it is possible that 75% of all large, indigenous mammals, including elephants, giant ground sloths, and camels, died out at our hands. The death of these "keystone species" is also said to have changed the world's vegetation.

Many of the remaining mammals found it unsuitable and so were to disappear, too. Only time will tell if, at the start of the 21st century, we can act wisely to cut short the sixth extinction without causing further ecological chaos.

WIPEOUT

Pterosaurs, like the one *right,* became extinct during the fifth mass extinction, 65 million years ago, along with the dinosaurs.

THE NEWCOMERS

While the 21st-century world wakes up at last to the importance of conservation of plant and animal life, previously unknown species continue to be discovered with surprising regularity all over the planet. Some are even created entirely by accident.

With some of the physical characteristics of a zebra and some of a giraffe, and a very long blue tongue, the okapi hit the headlines. It still exists in the wild, and there are now specimens in many zoos. But perhaps it is not nearly so extraordinary as a recently discovered octopus.

One of the most exciting zoological discoveries of the 20th century, the okapi of Zaire, Africa, is a type of short-necked giraffe that had been known to the pygmy people who shared its forest habitat, but had never been officially named or studied.

By all accounts it had a partly striped, rich brown coat, and cloven hooves. It was also said to be very shy. The native population caught it for its delicious flesh by digging pits into which it would stumble.

All this was hearsay until in 1901 it was found and described by Sir Harry Johnston, who likened its smooth coat to velvet and remarked on its pale, almost ghostlike face. But specimens captured by the New York Zoological Society in 1915 failed to survive.

A LOVING LICK
Okapis, not discovered by anyone from outside Africa until the early 20th century, show their affection both to a mate and to their young by licking their faces.

WELCOME TO THE FAMILY!
Known as a ligron, the animal *above* is a cross between a lion and a tiger, as you can see from its body shape and markings. As such it is a new member of the cat family.

QUICK-CHANGE ARTIST

This octopus has yet to be named, but scientists are already staggered by the skill with which it can mimic several poisonous sea creatures in order to stop predators. It is in effect a master of disguise.

One moment, for instance, it resembles a lion fish; the next it changes color and looks just like a poisonous yellow-and-black-striped sea snake. Many creatures use camouflage to protect themselves and may take on one particular guise to hide themselves, but such an extensive repertoire is entirely out of the ordinary.

Recently, too, a new species of camel has been found in a remote region of Tibet. Remarkably, it has adapted to survive on salt water.

It is thought to be a species of camel never domesticated by humans and to have survived because it inhabits a remote area that, ironically, for many years was used by China for testing nuclear weapons. In 1996 these tests ended, but since then the camels have been killed for their meat in the most savage way imaginable. Landmines are placed by salt water springs so that when the camels come to quench their thirst, they are killed outright by the explosion. Only about 1,000 of these camels are now thought to exist.

New plants, too, continue to make an appearance. Some are simply beautiful and a source of fascination for the world's botanists. Other plants may not be so attractive but could have vital medicinal properties that may yet help scientists eliminate a number of the world's deadliest diseases. A new species of Brazilian mushroom, for example, is being studied in Japan, and early research shows it could

well have a part to play in curing some types of cancer. With so many species disappearing, thankfully others continue to be discovered for the first time.

Fact file

● Newly discovered creatures may be called by common names – megamouth, for example, is a shark first found off Hawaii in 1976 – but they also need to be classified scientifically. Scientific names are always given in Latin so that they can be recognized internationally, according to a system devised by the 18th-century Swedish naturalist Carl Linnaeus. The scientific name for megamouth is *Megachasma pelagios* (MEG-AK-AS-MAH PEL-AH-GEE-OS).

● New animals are often named because of their physical characteristics or after their discoverers. But those who name new creatures may have a sense of humor. There is a beetle, for example, named *Agra vation* (AG-RA-VAY-SHUN.)

A CROSS-BREED
New species may sometimes be bred unintentionally. During the summer of 2001, for example, a donkey was left in a field with a zebra. They mated, and this photograph shows their offspring.

REDISCOVERIES

Every now and then zoologists surprise us with the rediscovery of animals once thought extinct. The golden hamster – many millions of which flourish throughout the world as popular pets today – is probably the most famous example.

A CHANCE FIND

Although known in ancient times, golden hamsters remained elusive for thousands of years. But if you or some of your friends have one as a pet, you can be sure it is descended from the few found in Syria in 1930.

The story of the rediscovery of the golden hamster is a remarkable one. Professor Israel Aharoni of the Hebrew University in Jerusalem had noticed references in ancient manuscripts to the keeping of tame, mouselike creatures as pets by children living long ago in the region of Aleppo, Syria. However, even though he was a zoologist, he knew of no animal that fitted the description. But visiting the area in the attempt to find out more about this species, he had an an amazing stroke of luck.

SITTING PRETTY
Sometimes severely endangered species, such as the Hawaiian geese *above*, can be saved by captive breeding.

In a deep burrow that he chanced to explore were a female and several of her babies. No adult male could be found, however. Some of the young were bought back to Jerusalem, and three survived – a male and two females. Fortunately, they had no trouble breeding while in captivity, and Professor Aharoni also had the foresight to send a few of them to zoos throughout the world to ensure survival of the species as far as possible.

Other creatures reported to have ceased to exist have been rediscovered in even more curious ways. The world's largest beetle – the Titan longhorn that can grow up to 8 inches long, for instance – was rediscovered in the stomach of a large Brazilian fish just as it was being gutted. And the cahow – a small petrel native to Bermuda, a favorite prey of the black rat and thought extinct since the 17th century – was found in a secret breeding place on a nearby island.

DISAPPEARING ACT

Sometimes animals and birds thought to be extinct turn up out of the blue for a while, only to disappear again. The world's tiniest pygmy hog, just 2 feet long and no more than 12 inches high, for instance, had once been fairly common in the foothills of the Himalayas; but by the 1950s it was no longer to be seen, probably due to destruction of its habitat when local swampland was drained.

From time to time there were unconfirmed sightings, yet no one had provided any conclusive evidence. Then, in 1971 a few adults and young were positively identified in Assam, India. However, breeding them in captivity was not successful. So for the moment naturalists hope a number are still lurking in some remote area, awaiting rediscovery for a second time.

But what of creatures thought to have become extinct way back in prehistoric times? Do they sometimes reappear?

It is a rare occurrence, but it does happen. One example is the coelacanth, which you can read about in the volume in this set entitled *Extinct Underwater Life*. Another is *Neoglyphes inopinata* (NEE-OH-GLEYE-FAYZ IN-OP-IN-AH-TAH) – rediscovered in July 1908 in the South China Sea at a considerable depth. A type of shellfish, pink in color, with large eyes, and an ancestor of today's crabs, it was thought to have died out 50 million years ago. The second part of its scientific name, meaning "unexpected," is certainly very apt! The world of wildlife, as you can see, is full of the most amazing surprises.

IN DANGER TODAY

One hundred years ago there were 100,000 tigers in India, but today there are fewer than 3,000. Worse, they may be just five years from extinction. Who is to blame for the tragic decline in these big cats? And which other creatures are similarly affected?

International wildlife crime is increasingly a matter of concern. Indeed, as a disturbing United Nations report revealed in April 2000, ruthless poachers continue to kill rare species and smuggle out skins, shells, and horns for rich rewards in spite of existing bans.

SAVE THE TIGER!
This magnificent beast has long been hunted for its skin and body parts, thought by some to have medicinal properties or to be lucky charms.

In a single raid, for instance, wildlife inspectors found and seized seven tiger pelts, more than 100 claws, and 400 pounds of bones.

But there are instances when such horrific slaughter cannot be put down to personal greed. Top-secret national interests have also been known to affect some of the world's most endangered species.

HUNTED FROM ON HIGH
In spite of regulations forbidding the slaughter of polar bears, hundreds are still killed each year by those who know they can get a good price for their skins. When a plane flies low and a poacher aims accurately, there is little chance of escape for these Arctic creatures.

BYE-BYE TO THE AYE-AYE?
Destruction of its forest habitat on the island of Madagascar during the last half of the 20th century has led to a severe decline in the aye-aye, a type of lemur.

FATAL ACCIDENTS
Many Caribbean manatees, like the one seen underwater *left*, perish with alarming regularity due to collisions with boats.

Experts think the sounds disorientated these deep-diving whales and made them go totally crazy, so that they ended up ashore and were unable to return to the ocean.

One of the most endangered birds in West Africa, meanwhile, is the white-breasted guinea fowl. Its jungle habitat is fast disappearing, and it is regularly killed by poachers for its meat, in spite of being an officially protected species. The Jentink's duiker, an antelope from the same region, is severely threatened too.

The Japanese crane, the Atlantic walrus, the Arabian oryx, spectacled bears – these are just a few of the hundreds of species facing an uncertain future at the beginning of the 21st century. A lot is being

In the year 2000, for example, fourteen rare beaked whales were found beached in the Bahamas, and eight died. These whales are elusive creatures, and multiple deaths are unknown. What, then, could have caused this? Environmentalists think the underwater testing of an anti-submarine warfare system may possibly have confused the whales' normal navigational abilities through use of low-frequency sonic devices.

Fact file

- The International Union for Conservation of Nature and Natural Resources regularly publishes what is known as the *Red List*. The color here stands for "danger," and the list cites those creatures extinct or going into rapid decline.

- There may be as few as 700 giant pandas remaining in the wild, and the Worldwide Fund for Nature has this animal as its emblem.

- Many charities have been set up internationally to raise money for the support of specific endangered species.

- Zoos are sometimes criticized for keeping animals in captivity, but their contribution to the breeding and saving of endangered species is an important one.

done at an international level in the attempt to save them, but conservation can be time-consuming and costly, though certainly worthwhile and often very successful.

A DARK FUTURE?
In 1960 there were between 11,000 and 13,500 black rhinos in Africa. The estimate in 2001, however, stood at only 2,700.

43

SAVING THE SPECIES

Many bodies have been set up to protect our planet's endangered plants and animals and reintroduce them to the wild. How do they go about such conservation work? And are such efforts worthwhile?

Sometimes animals die out because, once their population has started to decrease, there are fewer available mates. As a result inbreeding occurs, causing general ill health and even abnormalities in the offspring. To avoid this, conservationists need to find new breeding partners with similar genetic makeup for the endangered species.

Take the Florida cougar. It became scarce and isolated due to hunting, destruction of its natural habitat, environmental pollution, and shortage of prey. But a limited number of Texas cougars – close relatives – have now been introduced to the range of the Florida cougar as part of a government program. In such an instance the aim is that successful mating of the two subspecies will reverse any previous negative effect of inbreeding.

TAKING REFUGE
The Florida cougar *above* – also known as a puma, panther, or mountain lion – was once widely hunted by farmers who were anxious to protect their livestock. Now very few remain, but they are protected within the Everglades National Park.

GETTING BETTER
Even the hideous Gila monster, *left*, from the southwestern United States and Mexico, and poisonous to other animals, should not be allowed to become extinct. Preliminary research has shown its secretions might be useful in treating a form of human diabetes. We find cures in the most unexpected places.

Thousands of California condors once flew the skies of western North America. But many perished as a result of eating poisoned coyote meat or the lead shot left in deer by hunters. Sadly, by the mid-1970s there were thought to be just fifty left in the wild. Conservationists stepped in, however, and took eggs from one of the last remaining nests. They were hatched artificially at the San Diego Zoo and then released into the wild.

PULLING THE TRIGGER

But why should we bother to save the many endangered species? Would it really matter if a large proportion of them simply disappeared? What we need to remember is that the billions of organisms living on our planet interact in complex ways. What is more, if certain keystone species go into decline or vanish, that can have a remarkable trigger effect. Once, for example, sea otters – a keystone species – were intensively hunted for their fur. When they eventually became endangered, the sea urchins, formerly their principal prey, greatly increased in number and began to consume huge quantities of kelp. In no time some of the ocean bed became desertlike, and other creatures normally reliant on kelp suffered in turn. We should on no account dismiss the importance of conservation when it comes to insects either.

TIGER BONE WINE

Tiger bone wine is sold as a tonic in Chinese communities around the world. These bottles were found in a Chinese supermarket in Central London during Operation Charm.

BEASTLY BEVERAGE
How many endangered tigers had to die unnecessarily to make the illegal tiger bone wine, *above*, confiscated by police in London, England?

One scientist even has a theory that if all insects and other creepy-crawlies were to disappear tomorrow, we humans would not survive for longer than a few months.

Many endangered plants are simply beautiful in their own right. Some, though, might also hold important secrets. At present about a quarter of all medicines are derived from plants, and research may well show that a lot more have vital curative properties.

Whether or not we humans even survive as a species could ultimately depend on careful conservation of our plants. The shape of tomorrow's world will undoubtedly be a reflection of the action we take today.

BRINGING BACK THE BALD EAGLE
Water pollution, hunting, and widespread use of pesticides combined to severely endanger America's national bird. However, action on the part of conservationists has increased numbers to such an extent there are now about 50,000 living in the wild.

GLOSSARY

AIDS
a disease spread by the HIV virus either through blood or sexually, causing damage to the immune system, and for which there is no known cure as yet

CFCs
an abbreviation for Chlorofluorocarbons (KLOR-OH-FLOOR-OH-KAR-BONS) that are harmful greenhouse gases mostly produced by aerosol sprays, refrigerators, and air conditioners

coniferous
trees, such as pine and firs, that bear cones

conservation
preservation of the environment

deciduous
losing its leaves in autumn

ecology
the study of plants and animals in relation to the environment

epidemic
a widely spreading outbreak of disease

erosion
wearing away

evolution
the development of higher forms of life out of lower forms

geologist
a scientist who studies the structure of the Earth

habitat
the natural environment of an animal or plant

lava
a hot emission from an erupting volcano

malaria
a disease spread by mosquitoes

mutations
changes

ozone
a form of oxygen harmful in concentrations and forming a protective layer in the atmosphere that shields us from the Sun

paleontologist
a scientist who studies fossils

pelt
an animal's fur or skin

permafrost
permanently frozen soil

Permian times
a period lasting from about 280 to 230 million years ago

photosynthesis
the interaction and absorption of light, water, and carbon dioxide to produce healthy green plants

plate tectonics
the study of processes by which Earth has reached its present form

Precambrian times
prior to 570 million years ago

pygmy
a small animal or small race of human beings

spawning
producing or depositing eggs

symbiosis
a close relationship between two interdependent animal or plant species

Triassic times
a period lasting from about 249 to 213 million years ago

tundra
a treeless landscape with permanently frozen soil

ultraviolet light
part of the light spectrum that, in excess, can be harmful to animal life

virus
a cause of infection or disease